Max Takes the Train

by Rosemary Wells
illustrated by Jody Wheeler

Editorial Offices: Glenview, Illinois • Parsippany, New Jersey • New York, New York

Sales Offices: Needham, Massachusetts • Duluth, Georgia • Glenview, Illinois
Coppell, Texas •Sacramento, California • Mesa, Arizona

Zeke's Palace of Ice Cream ran a special on their double chocolate ice cream Whamburger with coconut curls and red sprinkles.

Max wanted one.

"No, Max," said Max's sister, Ruby.

"Zeke's Palace of Ice Cream is too far away."

But Uncle Bunny said, "Let's go!"

Max put his Junior Citizen Transport Pass
around his neck, and they went out and waited
for the bus at the bus stop sign.

A big red bus came along.
Putt, putt, putt! went the bus.

The bus went into the city center,
but it did not pass Zeke's Palace of Ice Cream.

Max and Uncle Bunny got off the bus.
"Where to?" asked Uncle Bunny. Max saw the sign
for the Blue Comet Express. They went up the
escalator and boarded the Blue Comet.

Choo, choo, choo! went the Blue Comet.

The train passed houses and farms.
But it did not go to Zeke's Palace of Ice Cream.

Max and Uncle Bunny hopped off the train.
Max spotted a sign for the ferryboat.
They boarded the ferryboat.

Chugga, chugga, chugga! went the ferryboat.
The ferryboat crossed the lake. But it did not go to
Zeke's Palace of Ice Cream.

On the other side of the lake was a sign for
Air-O-Zoom. Max and Uncle Bunny followed the
arrows down the jetway.

They took seats on the plane. They fastened their seatbelts and made sure their tray-tables were in the upright position. "Coffee, tea, or milk?" asked the flight attendant.

Max did not want coffee, tea, or milk.
He wanted the chocolate Whamburger.
Zoom, zoom, zoom! went the plane.

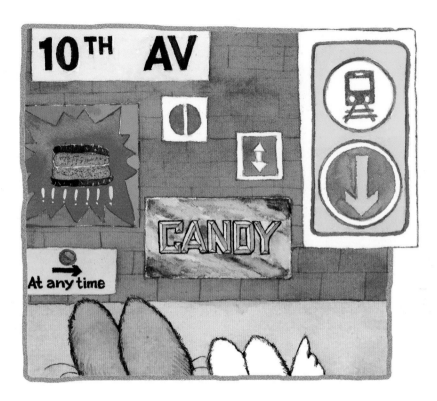

But the plane did not land at Zeke's Palace of
Ice Cream. In the airport there was a sign for the
Metro Subway Liner.

Max and Uncle Bunny went down, down, down,
underground into the subway tunnel. They chose the
Yellow line. They minded the gap and the closing doors.
Clicka, clicka, clicka! went the Metro Subway Liner.

16

The subway came to its first stop. In the station
was a picture of a double chocolate Whamburger
with coconut curls and red sprinkles.
"Let's go!" said Uncle Bunny.

At the top of the steps was Zeke, large as life.
Max and Uncle Bunny put in their orders.
"Two double Whamburgers with the works!"
yelled Zeke.

But two double Whamburgers were too much
for Max and Uncle Bunny to finish.
"We had better call Ruby!" said Uncle Bunny.

On the back of Max's Junior Citizen Transport Pass was his telephone number. Max dialed it.

Ruby answered. "Where are you?" asked Ruby.
"At Zeke's," said Max.

Ruby attached the sidecar to her Bicycle
Built for Two. She rode all the way to Zeke's
Palace of Ice Cream without stopping.

Zeke kept the Whamburger cold for Ruby.
But even Ruby couldn't finish it.

They all got on the Bicycle Built for Two with the
sidecar and brought the rest of the Whamburger
back to Grandma.